ILLUMINATIONS FROM THE BHAGAVAD-GĪTĀ

ILLUMINATIONS FROM THE

Kim and Chris Murray

Foreword by Satsvarūpa dāsa Gosvāmī

HARPER COLOPHON BOOKS
Harper & Row, Publishers
New York, Cambridge, Hagerstown, Philadelphia, San Francisco
London, Mexico City, São Paulo, Sydney

BHAGAVAD-GĪTĀ

Grateful acknowledgment is made to Bhaktivedanta Book Trust for permission to reprint excerpts from *Bhagavad-Gītā As It Is* by His Divine Grace A.C. Bhaktivedanta Swami Prabhupāda. Copyright © 1972 by Bhaktivedanta Book Trust. For information address Bhaktivedanta Book Trust, 3764 Watseka Avenue, Los Angeles, California 90034.

FIRST EDITION

Designed by Kim Llewellyn

LIBRARY OF CONGRESS CATALOG CARD NUMBER: 79-3834
ISBN: 0-06-090763-0
80 81 82 83 84 10 9 8 7 6 5 4 3 2 1

Contents

Preface

HAGAVAD-GĪTĀ is like the sun, shining for everyone. It is not a sectarian doctrine, meant for a particular faith or class of people. It is the Song of God, meant for the enlightenment of us all. *Bhagavad-gītā* is the essence of all Vedic literature. "Veda" means knowledge, and Lord Kṛṣṇa, the original knower of the *Vedas*, is the author of *Bhagavad-gītā*. By studying this transcendental literature we are learning from Kṛṣṇa himself. Kṛṣṇa declares in the *Gītā* that "he who studies this sacred conversation worships Me by his intelligence."

Though first spoken long ago, *Bhagavad-gītā* remains utterly vital today. It is not sentimental but is practical—a handbook of wisdom for our troubled times. Arjuna was experiencing many difficulties on the Battlefield of Kurukṣetra. Today, we are likewise burdened with many serious problems. War, poverty, pollution, and greed are everywhere, and getting worse. This is an age of anxiety. But the heart of the Lord is mercy, and, in *Bhagavad-gītā*, Kṛṣṇa gives us the knowledge by which our activities may be purified and our suffering mitigated. If a person is interested to increase his own happiness and that of society at large, the *Gītā* can show the way. Kṛṣṇa spoke *Bhagavad-gītā* to take us from the darkness of ignorance to the light of knowledge—to illuminate us.

This book is a celebration of the glory of *Bhagavad-gītā* and its author, Lord Kṛṣṇa. Presented is a selection of verses from the *Gītā* (which one should read in entirety to fully relish its sublime philosophy) and a series of illustrations depicting some of Kṛṣṇa's wonderful pastimes and activities.

Kṛṣṇa's nature is transcendent. He is the Supreme Beauty who resides in everyone's heart. His form is all attractive and unlimited. In the spiritual world, love rules supreme. It is by love and devotion that Kṛṣṇa may be known. This is the natural function of the soul. In such spirit, this book is offered to Kṛṣṇa and to his intimate devotee, His Divine Grace A. C. Bhaktivedanta Swami Prabhupāda, and his followers. If this book gives them some transcendental pleasure, then our efforts are a success.

We wish to acknowledge the appreciation and encouragement of our friends for this project. Our special thanks go to R. D. Scudellari; to our editor, Hugh Van Dusen; and to our parents.

—KIM AND CHRIS MURRAY

Foreword

HE TIME is five thousand years ago. The scene is a battlefield at Kurukṣetra, India. A chariot bearing charioteer and archer sits between the opposing phalanxes of two mighty armies.

The battle which is about to begin is the inevitable climax of years of political intrigue. It is a fratricidal war to determine who will occupy the throne: righteous Yudhisthira, who is the eldest son of the dead King Pandu and the rightful heir, or his treacherous cousin, Duryodhana, who is trying to usurp the kingdom. Conchshells, bugles, and drums sound as two huge military forces poise for battle. From his chariot between the armies, the archer, Arjuna, beholds the soldiers on the enemy's side—many of whom are his own relatives—and he becomes overwhelmed with compassion and familial affection. Weeping, he lays down his weapons and refuses to fight.

At this point *Bhagavad-gītā* begins. Arjuna humbles himself before his chariot driver, who we learn is no ordinary charioteer but the Supreme Personality of Godhead Himself, Lord Kṛṣṇa. Accepting Lord Kṛṣṇa as his spiritual master, Arjuna asks for help in his moment of crisis, and for one hour the world stands still as the Lord instructs Arjuna, and subsequently all mankind, in the wisdom of *Bhagavad-gītā*, the Song of God.

The Supreme Lord said: While speaking learned words, you are mourning for what is not worthy of grief. Those who are wise lament neither for the living nor the dead. Never was there a time when I did not exist, nor you, nor all these kings; nor in the future shall any of us cease to be.

Thus a momentous dialogue ensues as Lord Kṛṣṇa explains the science of the spiritual soul, the material nature, and the Supreme Personality of Godhead, who controls both the spiritual and the material. Lord Kṛṣṇa says: "I shall now declare to you in full this knowledge both phenomenal and noumenal, by knowing which there shall remain nothing further to be known."

Today, fifty centuries later, *Bhagavad-gītā* remains the world's most complete book of scientific spiritual knowledge. Within India's great treasure house of human understanding, the Vedic literature, *Bhagavad-gītā* is perennially the most popular book. In the West, the *Gītā* has had profound influence on philosophy and literature and has been studied by virtually all our major thinkers for the past two hundred years.

The present volume, *Illuminations from the Bhagavad-gītā,* is appropriately titled, since the *Gītā*'s teachings are indeed illuminating. As one verse says: "When one is enlightened with the knowledge by which nescience is destroyed, then his knowledge reveals everything, as the sun lights up everything in the daytime."

That these verse translations are taken from *Bhagavad-gītā As It Is,* by His Divine Grace A. C. Bhaktivedanta Swami Prabhupāda, makes the book doubly illuminating. A shroud of mystical jargon, which is nothing more than imprecise, impersonal rhetoric, obscures most English translations of the *Gītā,* but here the translations are refreshingly lucid—illuminating. The reader comes away enriched with the wisdom of *Bhagavad-gītā,* not puzzled by riddles. These illuminations, designed and painted by Kim and Chris Murray, wed tastefully with each verse, as page after page radiates with the wisdom and beauty of *Bhagavad-gītā.*

Far more than just a picture book, these rich pages illumine many of the *Gītā*'s eternal truths. Here are a few of them.

The soul is eternal:

For the soul there is never birth nor death. Nor, having once been, does he ever cease to be. He is unborn, eternal, ever-existing, undying and primeval. He is not slain when the body is slain.

The soul is our permanent identity throughout this lifetime, and at death we transmigrate to another body:

As the embodied soul continually passes, in this body, from boyhood to youth to old age, the soul similarly passes into another body at death. The self-realized soul is not bewildered by such a change.

Lord Kṛṣṇa is the father of all souls, the source of creation, and the all-powerful controller:

Of all that is material and all that is spiritual in this world, know for certain that I am both its origin and dissolution.

I am the generating seed of all existences. There is no being—moving or unmoving—that can exist without Me.

Lord Kṛṣṇa's immanence can be perceived throughout His creation:

Know that all beautiful, glorious, and mighty creations spring from but a spark of My splendor.

Lord Kṛṣṇa, as the Supersoul, accompanies each transmigrating soul from one body to another:

The Supreme Lord is situated in everyone's heart, and is directing the wanderings of all living entities.

Lord Kṛṣṇa enlightens His worshippers from within their hearts:

Out of compassion for them [the constantly devoted souls], I, dwelling within their hearts, destroy with the shining lamp of knowledge the darkness born of ignorance.

He also enlightens these devoted souls from without through His representative, the spiritual master:

Just try to learn the truth by approaching a spiritual master. Inquire from him submissively and render service unto him. The self-realized soul can impart knowledge unto you because he has seen the truth.

Lord Kṛṣṇa, although immanent, is simultaneously situated transcendentally in the spiritual world of bliss and knowledge. And the transmigrating soul, after having been perfectly enlightened by Lord Kṛṣṇa (the Supersoul), the spiritual master, and *Bhagavad-gītā,* can also return to the spiritual world:

One who knows the transcendental nature of My appearance and activities does not, upon leaving the body, take his birth again in this material world, but attains My eternal abode.

—Satsvarūpa dāsa Gosvāmī

You cannot see Me with your present eyes.
Therefore I give you divine eyes, so that you can
behold My mystic opulence.

(Bhagavad-Gītā 11–8)

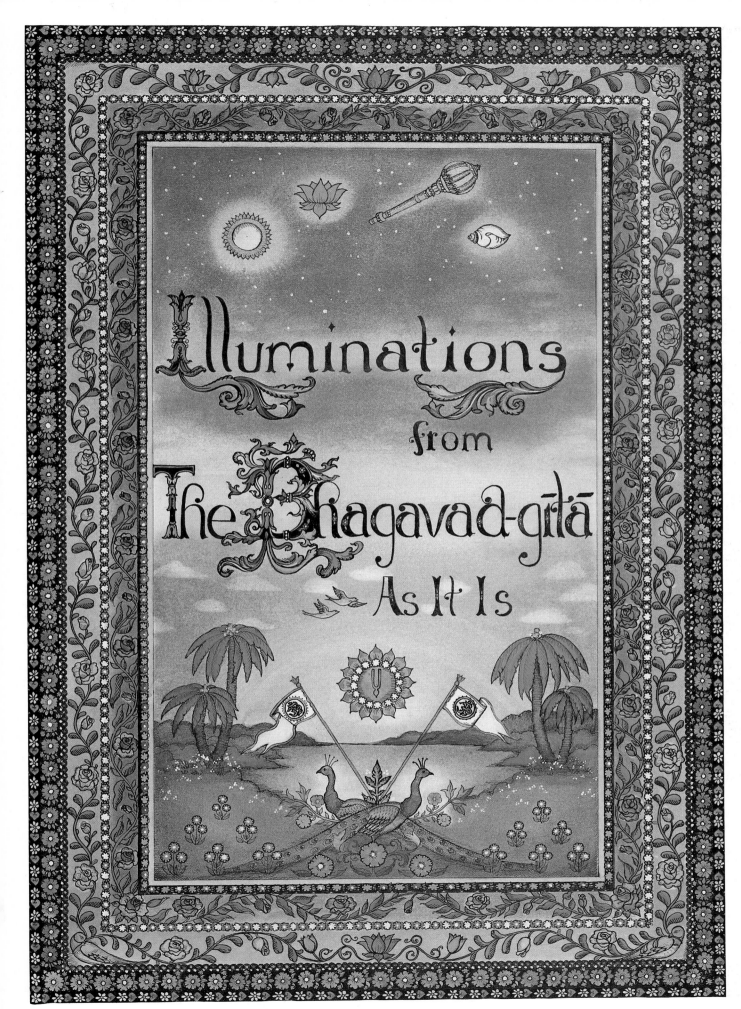

DEDICATION

TO

His Divine Grace

AC Bhaktivedanta Swami Prabhupāda

The greatest exponent of the Bhagavad-gita and its teachings in the western world.

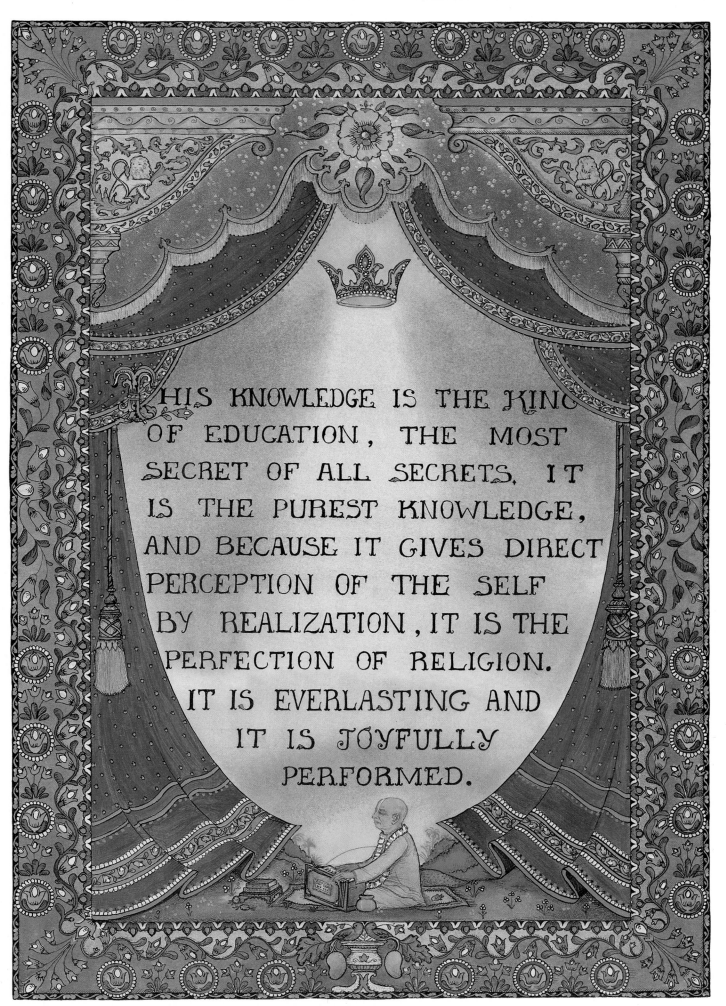

THIS KNOWLEDGE IS THE KING OF EDUCATION, THE MOST SECRET OF ALL SECRETS. IT IS THE PUREST KNOWLEDGE, AND BECAUSE IT GIVES DIRECT PERCEPTION OF THE SELF BY REALIZATION, IT IS THE PERFECTION OF RELIGION. IT IS EVERLASTING AND IT IS JOYFULLY PERFORMED.

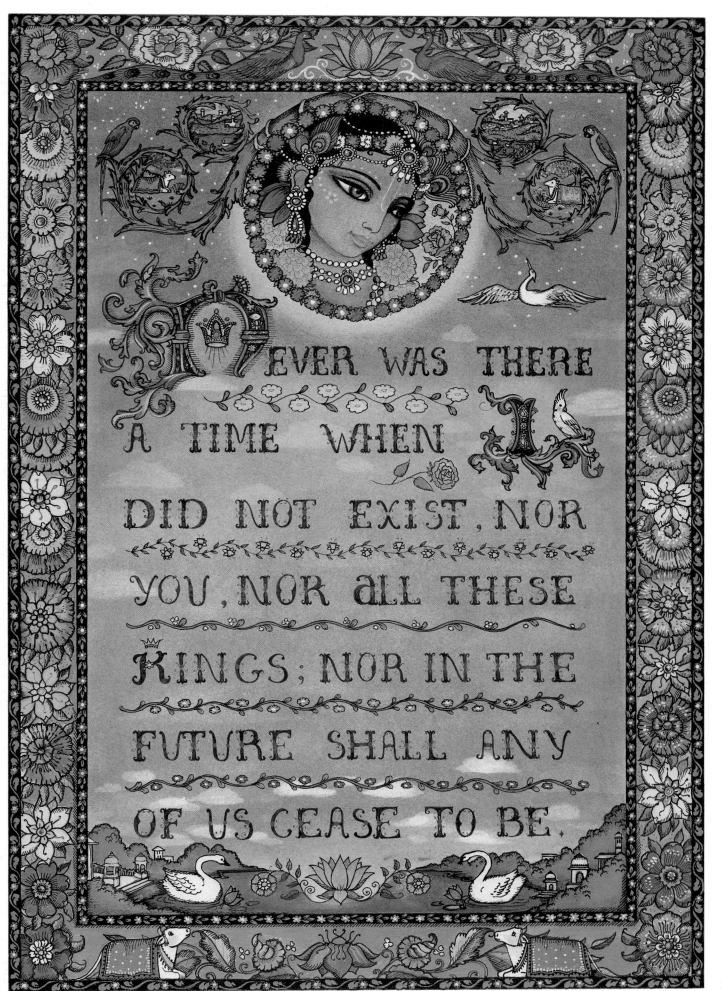

27

As the embodied soul continually passes, in this body, from boyhood to youth to old age, the soul similarly passes into another body at death.

The self realized soul is not bewildered by such a change.

For the soul there is never birth nor death nor, having once been, does he ever cease to be. He is unborn, eternal, ever-existing, undying and primeval. He is not slain when the body is slain.

31

33

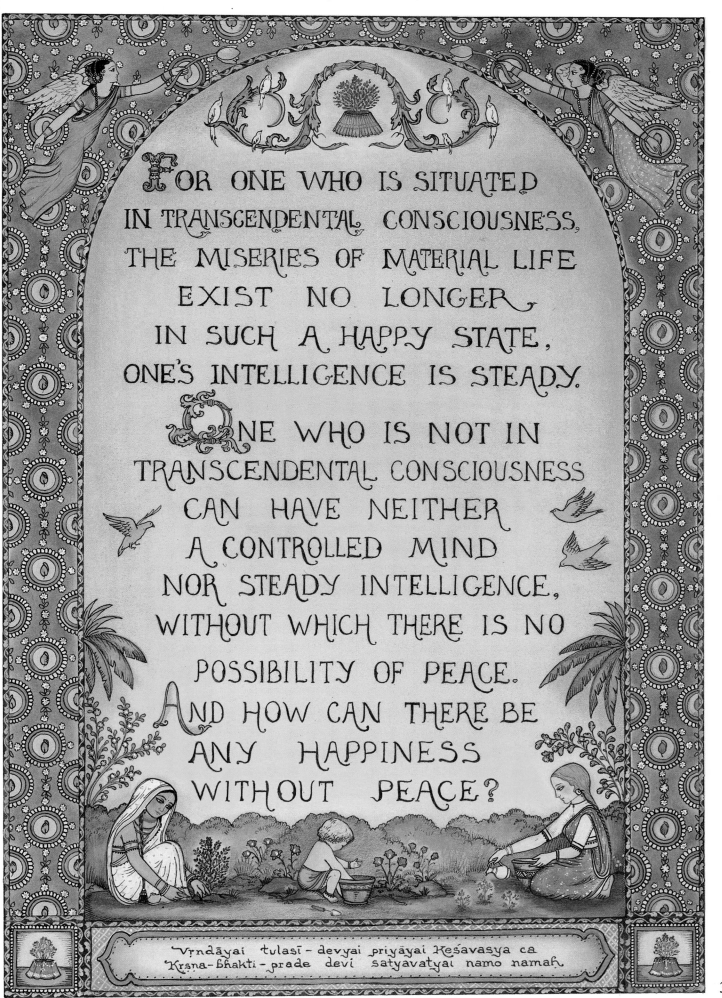

FOR ONE WHO IS SITUATED
IN TRANSCENDENTAL CONSCIOUSNESS,
THE MISERIES OF MATERIAL LIFE
EXIST NO LONGER
IN SUCH A HAPPY STATE,
ONE'S INTELLIGENCE IS STEADY.
ONE WHO IS NOT IN
TRANSCENDENTAL CONSCIOUSNESS
CAN HAVE NEITHER
A CONTROLLED MIND
NOR STEADY INTELLIGENCE,
WITHOUT WHICH THERE IS NO
POSSIBILITY OF PEACE.
AND HOW CAN THERE BE
ANY HAPPINESS
WITHOUT PEACE?

Vṛndāyai tulasī-devyai priyāyai Keśavasya ca
Kṛṣṇa-bhakti-prade devi satyavatyai namo namaḥ

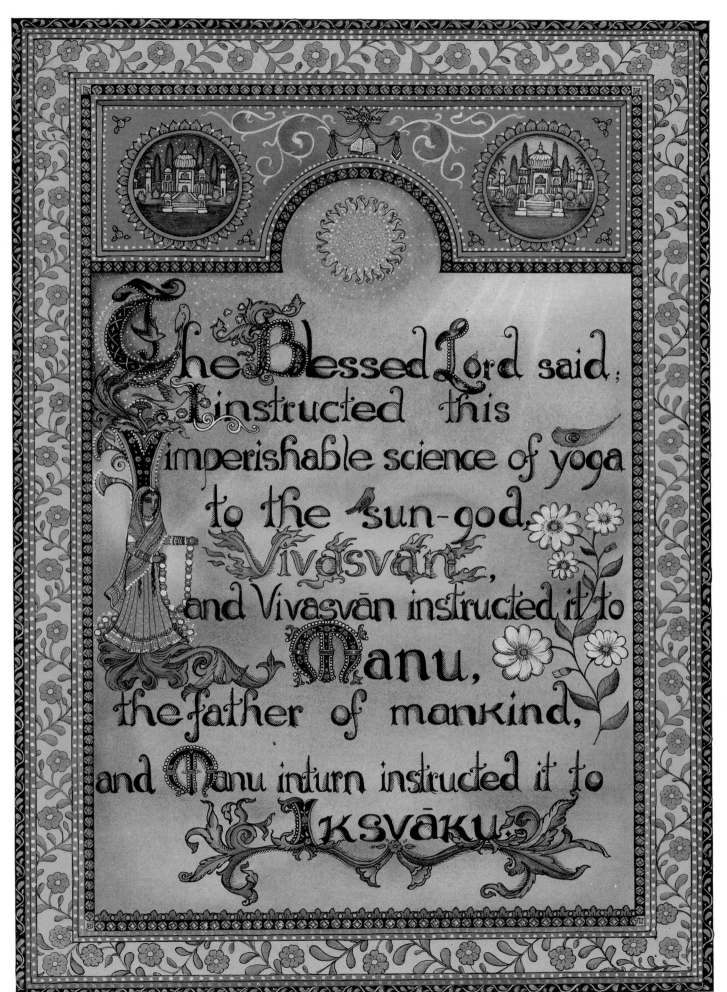

The Blessed Lord said; I instructed this imperishable science of yoga to the sun-god, Vivasvān, and Vivasvān instructed it to Manu, the father of mankind, and Manu in turn instructed it to Iksvāku.

39

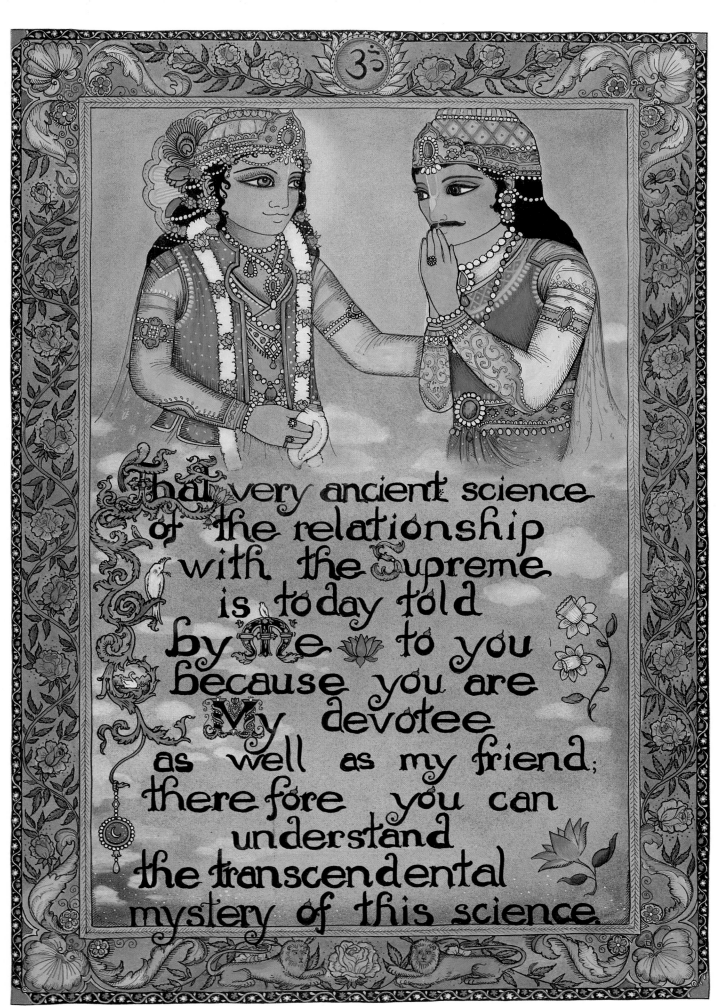

That very ancient science
of the relationship
with the Supreme
is today told
by Me to you
because you are
My devotee
as well as my friend;
therefore you can
understand
the transcendental
mystery of this science

43

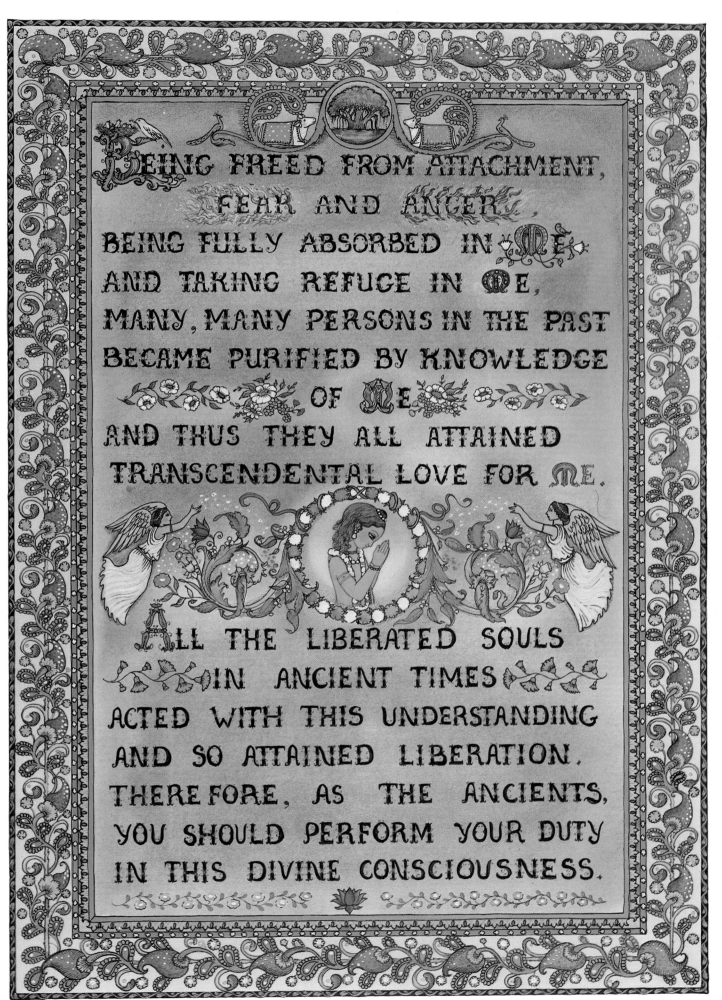

BEING FREED FROM ATTACHMENT, FEAR AND ANGER, BEING FULLY ABSORBED IN ME AND TAKING REFUGE IN ME, MANY, MANY PERSONS IN THE PAST BECAME PURIFIED BY KNOWLEDGE OF ME AND THUS THEY ALL ATTAINED TRANSCENDENTAL LOVE FOR ME.

ALL THE LIBERATED SOULS IN ANCIENT TIMES ACTED WITH THIS UNDERSTANDING AND SO ATTAINED LIBERATION. THEREFORE, AS THE ANCIENTS, YOU SHOULD PERFORM YOUR DUTY IN THIS DIVINE CONSCIOUSNESS.

JAYA JAGADISH HARE

47

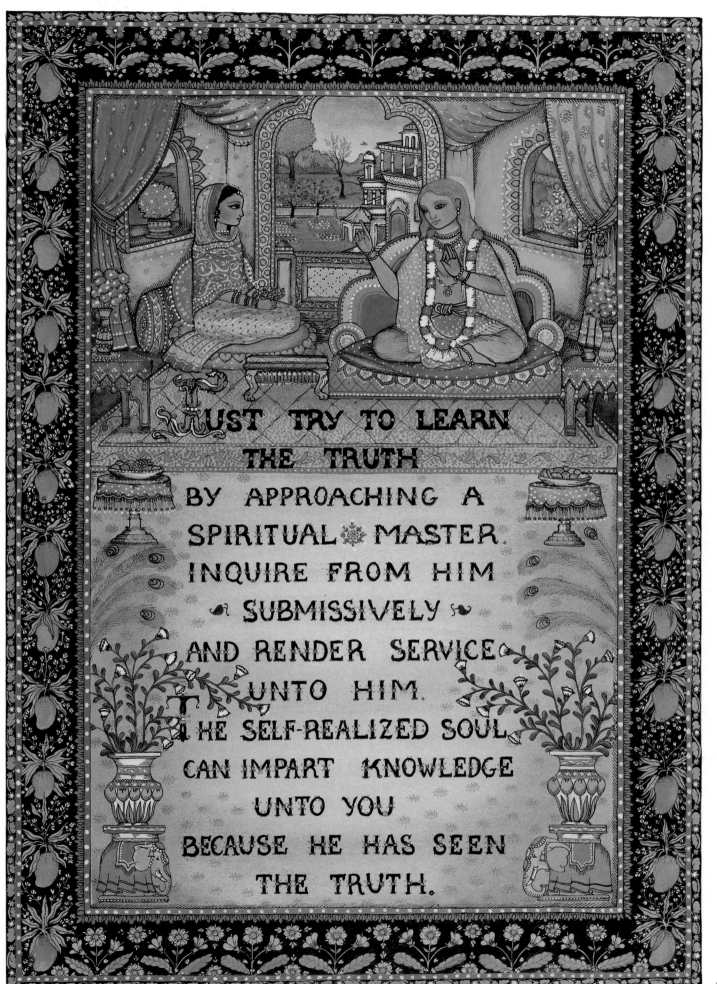

JUST TRY TO LEARN
THE TRUTH
BY APPROACHING A
SPIRITUAL MASTER.
INQUIRE FROM HIM
SUBMISSIVELY
AND RENDER SERVICE
UNTO HIM.
THE SELF-REALIZED SOUL
CAN IMPART KNOWLEDGE
UNTO YOU
BECAUSE HE HAS SEEN
THE TRUTH.

EVEN IF YOU ARE
CONSIDERED TO BE
THE MOST SINFUL
OF ALL SINNERS,
WHEN YOU ARE SITUATED
IN THE BOAT OF
TRANSCENDENTAL KNOWLEDGE,
YOU WILL BE ABLE
TO CROSS OVER
THE OCEAN OF MISERIES.

53

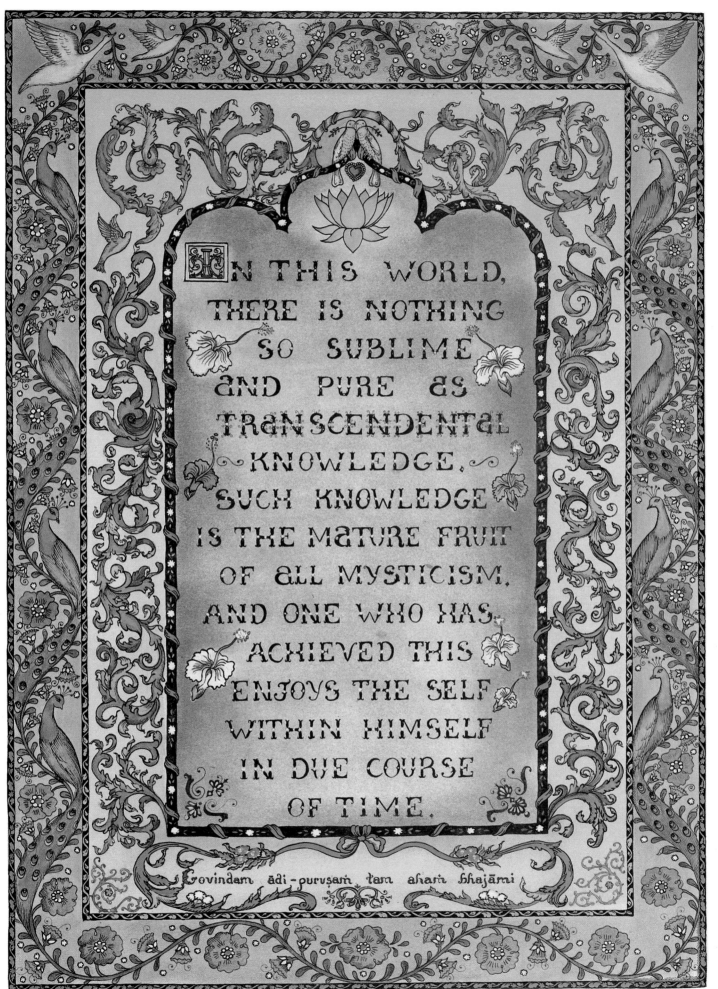

In this world, there is nothing so sublime and pure as transcendental knowledge. Such knowledge is the mature fruit of all mysticism, and one who has achieved this enjoys the self within himself in due course of time.

Govindam ādi-puruṣaṁ tam ahaṁ bhajāmi

57

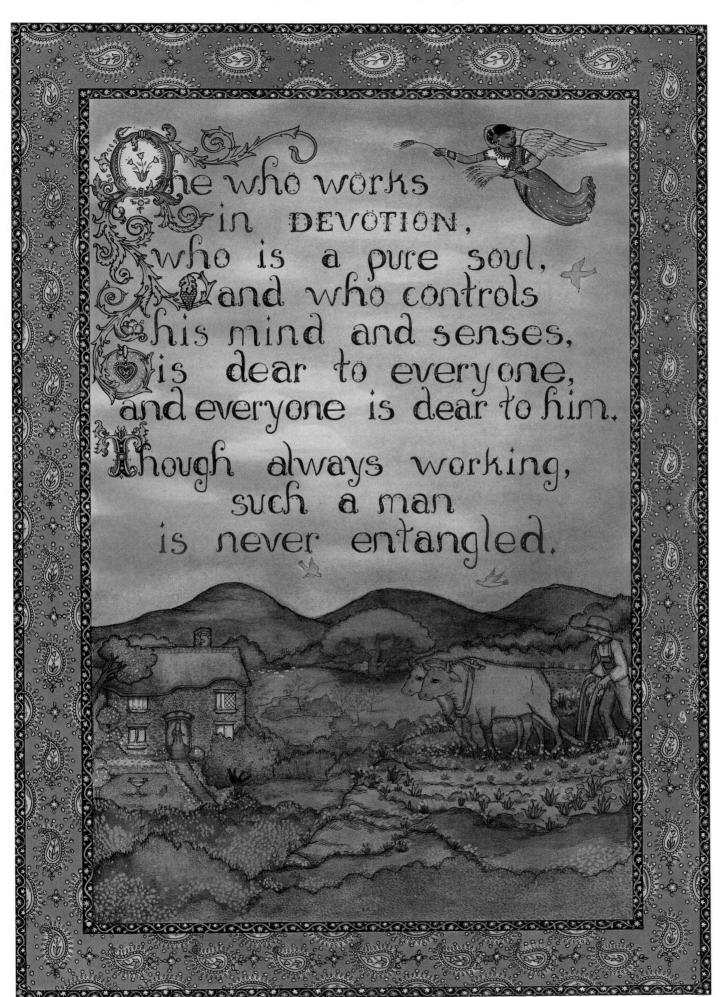

One who works in DEVOTION, who is a pure soul, and who controls his mind and senses, is dear to everyone, and everyone is dear to him.

Though always working, such a man is never entangled.

When one is enlightened
with the knowledge
by which nescience is destroyed,
then his knowledge reveals
every thing,
as the sun lights up
every thing
in the day time.

One whose happiness is within, who is active within, who rejoices within and is illumined within, is actually the perfect mystic. He is liberated in the Supreme, and ultimately he attains the Supreme

A MAN MUST ELEVATE HIMSELF
BY HIS OWN MIND,
NOT DEGRADE HIMSELF,
THE MIND IS THE FRIEND
OF THE CONDITIONED SOUL,
AND HIS ENEMY AS WELL.

FOR ONE WHOSE MIND
IS UNBRIDLED,
SELF-REALIZATION IS
DIFFICULT WORK.
BUT HE WHOSE MIND IS
CONTROLLED AND WHO STRIVES
BY RIGHT MEANS
IS ASSURED OF SUCCESS.

IF ONE OFFERS ME WITH LOVE
AND DEVOTION A LEAF,
A FLOWER, FRUIT OR WATER
WILL ACCEPT IT.

Oṁ ajñāna-timirandhasya jñānāñjana-śalākayā cakṣur unmīlitaṁ yena tasmai śrī-gurave namaḥ

TO THOSE WHO ARE CONSTANTLY DEVOTED AND WORSHIP ME WITH LOVE, I GIVE THE UNDERSTANDING BY WHICH THEY CAN COME TO ME.

OUT OF COMPASSION FOR THEM, I, DWELLING IN THEIR HEARTS, DESTROY WITH THE SHINING LAMP OF KNOWLEDGE THE DARKNESS BORN OF IGNORANCE.

Mānasa, deho, geho, yo kichu mora Arpiluṅ tuyā pade, Nanda-kiśora

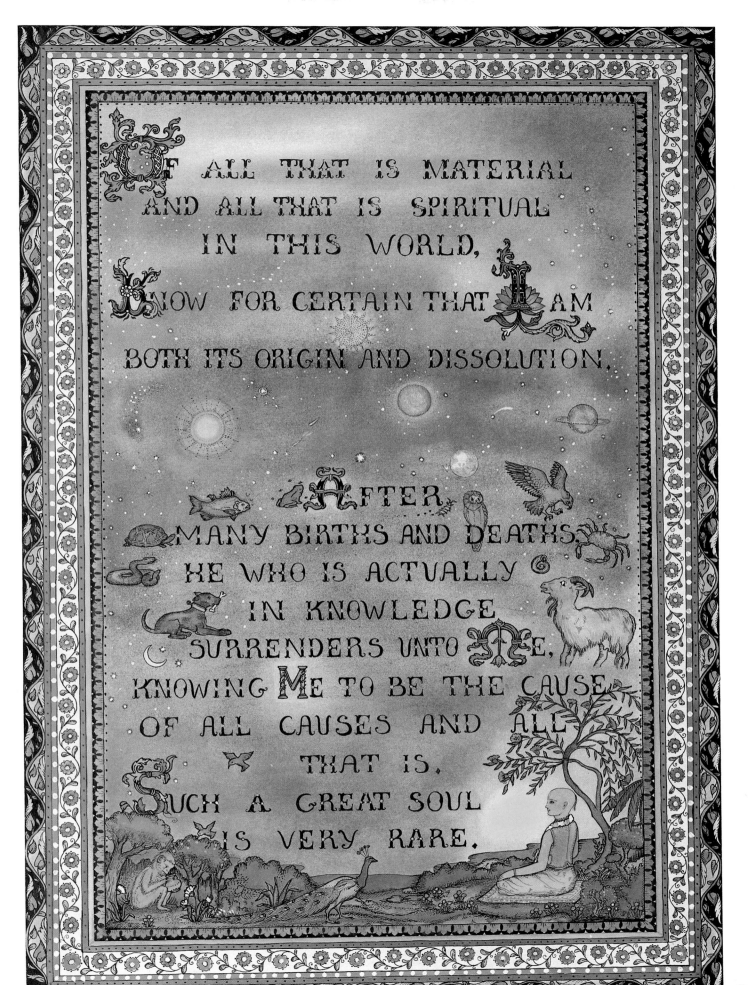

OF ALL THAT IS MATERIAL AND ALL THAT IS SPIRITUAL IN THIS WORLD, KNOW FOR CERTAIN THAT I AM BOTH ITS ORIGIN AND DISSOLUTION.

AFTER MANY BIRTHS AND DEATHS, HE WHO IS ACTUALLY IN KNOWLEDGE SURRENDERS UNTO ME, KNOWING ME TO BE THE CAUSE OF ALL CAUSES AND ALL THAT IS. SUCH A GREAT SOUL IS VERY RARE.

SHREEPAD SANATAN GOSWAMI PRABHUS BHAJAN KUTI

THE THOUGHTS OF MY PURE DEVOTEES DWELL IN ME, THEIR LIVES ARE SURRENDERED TO ME, AND THEY DERIVE GREAT SATISFACTION AND BLISS ENLIGHTENING ONE ANOTHER AND CONVERSING ABOUT ME.

79

I am the generating seed of all existences. There is no being moving or unmoving that can exist without Me.

Know that all beautiful, glorious, and mighty creations spring from but a spark of My splendor.

THE SUPREME LORD IS SITUATED IN EVERYONE'S HEART, AND IS DIRECTING THE WANDERINGS OF ALL LIVING ENTITIES. SURRENDER UNTO HIM UTTERLY AND BY HIS GRACE YOU WILL ATTAIN TRANSCENDENTAL PEACE AND THE SUPREME AND ETERNAL ABODE

89

Notes

About the Authors

Kim and Chris Murray live in Washington, D.C., where they have their studio and an art gallery, the Govinda Gallery. The Murrays have traveled extensively and have visited India twice, where they studied *Bhagavad-Gītā* and researched many of the illustrations for this book. They were influenced by a variety of artistic traditions that include classical Indian art, the great illuminated manuscripts, as well as nineteenth-century book design.

Kim Murray is a painter and sculptor who is currently completing illustrations for a children's book. Chris Murray is finishing his M.A. degree in the History of Religions and is the director of their gallery.